BAROSSA VALLEY SKETCHBOOK

Vor

Vielen Dank für ihre
Freundschaft

THE SKETCHBOOK SERIES

Adelaide
Adelaide Hills
Albany
Angaston
Auckland
Australian Horses
Australian Ships
Ballarat and Western Goldfields
Balmain
Barossa Valley
Bassendean and Guildford
Bathurst
Beechworth
Bendigo and Eastern Goldfields
Blue Mountains
Brighton
Brighton and Seacliff
Brisbane
Broken Hill
Bunbury and Busselton
Burra
Cairns
Canberra
Carlton and Parkville
Cedric Emanuel's Canberra
Cedric Emanuel's Melbourne
Cedric Emanuel's Paddington
Cedric Emanuel's Sydney
Cedric Emanuel's Sydney Harbour
Christchurch
Clare and District
Collins Street
Dandenong
Darling Downs
Darwin
Diamond Valley
Fiji
Frankston and Mount Eliza
Fremantle
Gawler
Geelong
Geraldton
Gippsland
Glenelg
Gold Coast and Green Mountains
Goulburn
Grampians
Hahndorf
Hawkesbury River
Hawthorn and Kew
Historic Buildings of Sydney
Historic Hobart
Hobart
Hunter's Hill
Illawarra
Ipswich

Kangaroo Island
Kelly Country
Kensington and Norwood
Launceston
Magill
Melbourne
Melbourne Churches and Schools
Mildura and Wentworth
Mitcham Village
Moonta, Wallaroo, Kadina
Mosman
Mount Gambier
National Trust (Victoria)
Newcastle and Hunter Valley
New England
Norfolk Island
North Adelaide
Northern Territory
Old Adelaide Hotels
Old Melbourne Hotels
Old Victorian Country Pubs
Paddington
Parramatta
Perth
Phillip Island
Port Adelaide
Port Arthur
Portland
Port Lincoln
Port Macquarie
Port Phillip Bay
Port Pirie
Riverboats
River Murray
River Yarra
The Rocks, Sydney
Richmond and East Melbourne
Rottnest Island
Second Melbourne
South East
Southern Highlands
Southern Vineyards
Sydney
Sydney Harbour
Tasmania
Tea Tree Gully
Toorak and South Yarra
Tropical Queensland
Victor Harbor and District
Watsons Bay
Wellington
West Australian Goldfields
Western District
Windsor
Yankalilla and District
Yorke Peninsula

BAROSSA VALLEY SKETCHBOOK

drawings by
JEANETTE McLEOD

text by
COLIN THIELE

RIGBY LIMITED • ADELAIDE • SYDNEY
MELBOURNE • BRISBANE • PERTH

First published 1968
Reprinted 1974
Reprinted 1977
Copyright © 1968 by Jeanette McLeod and Colin Thiele
Library of Congress Catalog Card Number 68-19603
National Library of Australia Card Number & ISBN 0 85179 355 X
All rights reserved

Wholly set up and designed in Australia
Printed in Hong Kong

Old Police Station out-building – Tanunda

CONTENTS

The Heritage . . . . . . *Page 7*

The Churches . . . . . . *Page 21*

The Winemakers . . . . . . *Page 36*

ACKNOWLEDGMENTS

The author and artist gratefully acknowledge the generous co-operation of the people of the Barossa Valley, particularly that given by Rev. H. F. W. Proeve, Mr Marcus Krieg, Mr Colin Angas, Mr Wyndham Hill Smith, Mr Rex Painter, Mr Frank Nicholls, Mr Ray Beckwith, Mr Mervin Harms, Mr H. Thumm, and Dr A. C. Behrndt. Without their help it would not have been possible to re-live the spirit of the Barossa so fully, so enjoyably, and —we hope—so authentically.

THE HERITAGE

The Barossa is not just a place. For over a hundred years it has been much more than that—a way of life, perhaps, an attitude of mind, a quality of spirit. It has been labour and music, church festival and vintage, worship, and the ringing of bells. Nobody born within earshot of that deep-toned tolling can ever forget the sound; it wrings the air, a sweet-sad note of joy and sorrow, a pain-joy, birth-marriage-death note as mellow as autumn sunlight. Out of the past, out of Silesian history, out of Lutheran conviction, it wells and flows over the Sunday valley.

The steeples dot the land. They spire upwards from the trees and vineyards, fields and clusters of buildings, like postcard pictures from the Rhine: Langmeil and Tabor, Ebenezer and Light Pass, Gnadenfrei, Bethany, Gruenberg, and a dozen more. And in the little steep-gabled churches that stand in the shadows of the towers much of the character of the Valley has been shaped and nurtured.

Not that the German heritage is the only component of the Barossa. Far from it. Some of the great wineries, some of the finest rural and commercial enterprises have been the work of others. From early times there was a leavening of English, Scottish, and Irish in its community life, and of Anglican, Methodist, Presbyterian, and Roman Catholic among its worshippers. But for three generations the predominant spirit of the Valley was German. Language, customs, religion, food, and dress were transplanted whole and remained largely undiluted. Only in fairly recent times has change finally eroded the old patterns of family and communal life. Sons and daughters have left home, have followed different vocations, have married "foreigners," have ceased to speak *Barossa Deutsch*—that quaintly inbred and

hybrid language evolved from a century of linguistic isolation. Industry, too, has started to gnaw at the peripheries: cement works, marble quarries, and gravel pits desecrate the landscape with dust and din.

Geographically the Valley, forty miles north-east of Adelaide, is not large—roughly twenty miles long and eight wide. Despite marginal undulations it has a unity of structure. And it certainly has a beauty all its own. Seen from Mengler's Hill it is a cradle, a coolamon, a generous German sausage, a halved bottle with its bottom upturned near Truro and its neck corked by Lyndoch. And with the green vineyards below and the mauve-blue hills to north and south, it is always a kind of Eden to those who know it.

Correctly the name is Barrosa, the Hill of Roses, so named by Colonel William Light after the site of one of the battles of the Peninsular War; but by a draughtsman's mistake the name was misspelled on an early map and the error has been allowed to stand. Historically, therefore, the hills are Barrosa and the Valley at its southern extremity is Lynedoch Vale, again named by Light (after a friend who fought beside him in the Peninsular War) and again misspelled.

The advent of the Germans is a well-known story. Harried by religious persecution at home, led in their migration by Pastor August Ludwig Christian Kavel, and befriended by George Fife Angas, they began arriving in South Australia

Strait Gate Lutheran Church

from 1838 onwards. The first German settlement in the Valley occurred in 1842 at Bethany (sometimes loosely referred to in early statements as Neuschlesien—New Silesia). It consisted of twenty-eight Lutheran families. A year later the settlement at Langmeil, from which Tanunda was to grow, was established a few miles away on the Para River, and from then on new groups and congregations began to dot the area. The proliferation of small churches, sometimes within slingshot of one another, sprang from various causes: argument and schism among themselves, the structure of their society back home, the advent of new shiploads or "waves" of migrants who settled as separate entities near their colleagues.

   Most of these first settlers came from peasant stock. The pattern of daily life—customs, food, dress, houses, festivals—therefore followed strongly traditional lines. Birth, baptism, confirmation, marriage, death—the main moments in the cycle of life—were recorded carefully in the big black family Bible which was generously provided with space for such entries, and which was read sonorously by the head of the house after every meal. Weddings, especially, were cause

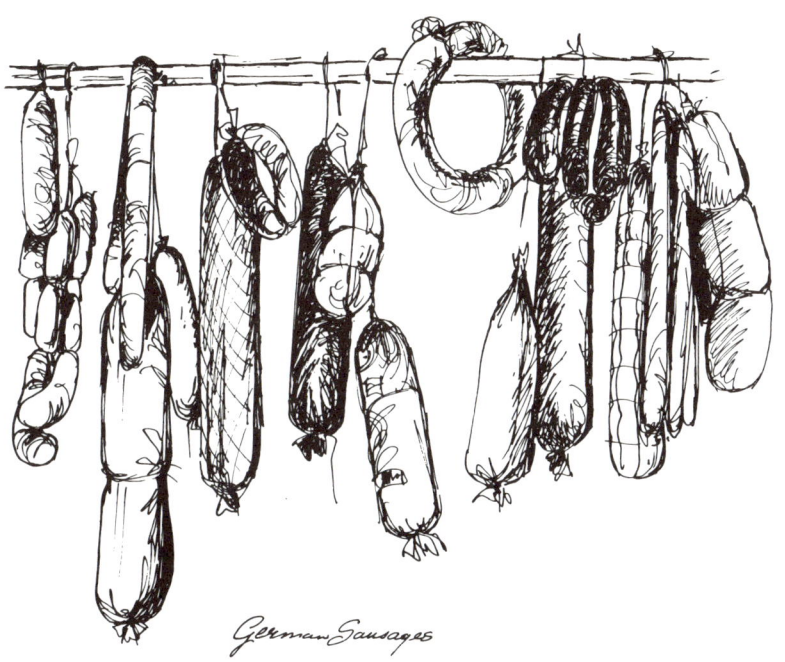

German Sausages

for prolonged celebration, preceded by tin-kettling and *Federschleissen* (communal stripping of feathers for the bridal mattress) and followed by gargantuan feasting. Brides wore black, as did mourners at funerals. Coffins were borne shoulder-high on a *Totenbahre* (funeral bier) by six bearers, and the whole procession was led to the graveside by a boy carrying a black wooden cross.

Dress was stern and conservative, language sober, festivals mainly religious. Food was distinctively "Continental" by English standards: *Sauerkraut* and *Sauer Gurken*, *Quarkkuchen* and *Quark Stinkerkäse*, home-made bread in rotund *Stollen*, *Pfannkuchen*, *Streuselkuchen* and *Honigkuchen*, and an incredible range of sausages. The killing of livestock for food, especially of steers and pigs, was often a community enterprise. On the *Schlachtentag* (slaughtering day) there was an inordinate stoking of fires and bubbling of cauldrons. For the sausage-makers the animal's stomach and intestines ("runners")

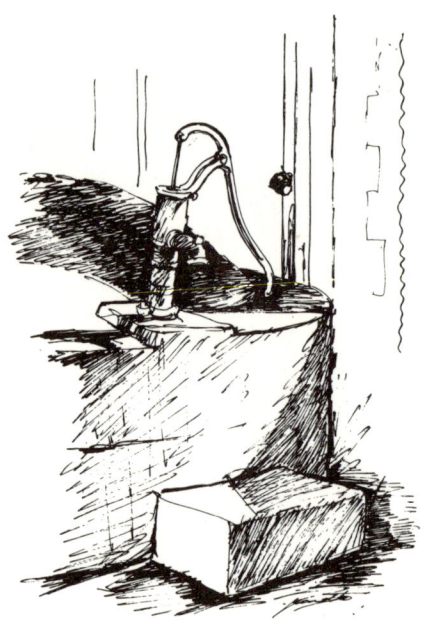

Underground tank at Ebenezer Church.

were flushed wholeheartedly with salt water and filled from a bin of sausage meat prepared and flavoured by the women, according to the nature of the sausage and the taste of the makers. It was high art. *Mettwurst, Blutwurst, Bratwurst,* and *Leberwurst* all went their way to the smokehouse or cellar with the *Speck* (bacon) and *Schinken* (ham).

Farm buildings were usually grouped around a yard—the house, sheds, stables, barn, and sties enclosing a kind of keep. The smoke-house usually adjoined the kitchen, and the bake-oven was a low igloo with a small door above or to the side of the kitchen fireplace. To this day some of the old smokehouse walls remain as brown as varnish from a century of smoke fires (wet sawdust or damp wood chips) necessary for curing bacons, hams, and smoked sausages.

Walls of houses and sheds were of timber and daub or stone and pug; roofs were of thatch. Hand-cut roofing beams,

Cottage in Billygoat Square - Tanunda.

lintels, and door-frames can still be seen in some of the old buildings, although lime mortar, galvanized iron, and sawn timber came into use as the resources of the settlers increased. Underground tanks with domed concrete roofs like heavy pill-boxes remain too, some of their hand-pumps still in use. There is still one near the vestry door at Ebenezer Church, with a concrete step so carefully placed that water falling from the pump just misses the edge. Members wanting a drink could not be expected to splash their boots before the service.

Farm implements were distinctive. The ubiquitous German waggon served as everything—family coach, hay cart, heavy transport, caravan, grape carrier, water cart, hearse, wedding chaise. It was impossible to imagine a family without one. Single-furrow hand ploughs, rollers fashioned from cylindrical tree trunks, scythes, winnowing forks, hoes, and garden tools were also universal. Seed was broadcast by hand and the sower walked stolidly up the furrow with the rhythm of centuries in his tread. The harvest was cut by scythe—a remarkable skill that brought the blade flashing within an inch of the ground, and laid out the swathe as neatly as a ruled line. Among many of the farmers its use continued long after Ridley's invention of the stripper. Indeed, innovation and change tended to be mistrusted; even in the twentieth century electricity, mechanical equipment, banks, radio, and refrigeration were accepted very slowly and with misgiving.

In the towns similar traditions prevailed. Tanunda has happily preserved some of its old buildings, especially

around the *Ziegenmarkt* (popularly called Billygoat Square). Here examples of early cottage design—thick walls, open beams, lime plaster—still remain, along with underground tank, hand pump, and the general pattern of the village market place. Town environment also allowed a more diverse social life in clubs and groups. Although the Barossa appears to have produced fewer *Schutzenverbände* (rifle-shooting clubs) than some of the other German settlements, it developed a reputation for music, singing, and marching, and at one time supported a renowned tea garden and skittle alley on the outskirts of Tanunda. Even today a skittle club still flourishes in the town.

BILLYGOAT SQUARE TANUNDA.

Individual eccentricities occasionally lightened the general tone of serious purpose and dour toil that marked the settlements. On New Year's Eve high spirited fellows hurried the old year out—especially if it had been a bad one—with the roar of double-barrelled blunderbusses. Old grandfather Braunack of Gomersal is reputed to have risen at four o'clock every morning and roused his family with a blast on a ram's horn loud enough to wake the sleeping and the dead. There were practical jokes, too, that fill the memories of the old people even now.

But for all that, entertainment in the Valley lay mainly in music and song. The Tanunda *Liedertafel* is almost as old as the town itself. A singing society, (*lieder* for songs, *tafel* for table) it was established in 1861 in the ancient round-the-table tradition of song, talk, and good fellowship. Coming from a background of community music-making and home entertainment, the early German singers transplanted the custom to South Australia where it has continued unbroken ever since—the oldest *Liedertafel* in Australia.

Rehearsing at the Liedertafel

A Bandsman at the Tanunda Band Competitions.

Characteristically the first members expected discipline. The inaugural constitution of 1861 laid down fines for unpunctuality (threepence if fifteen minutes late, sixpence if thirty) and a sixpenny penalty for leaving before ten o'clock. Membership was an honour—and it still is.

In its long history the *Liedertafel* has established a fine reputation for quality of singing and generosity of spirit. It has given concerts for charity in most parts of the State, and aided innumerable appeals. It has broadcast programmes frequently on radio and, more recently, on television. But most of all one likes to picture its members as men who meet simply for the love of music-making and companionship. In an age beset by pressure-pack music and instant entertainment, of the second-hand and the second-rate in admass civilization, it is good to preserve the joy of a common creative endeavour, and the genuine search after quality, which still characterizes the *Liedertafel*. Whether in rehearsal of a difficult concert song or in relaxed conversation during the break that follows, there is nothing ersatz here.

In the musical tradition of German family life men sang or played—or did both. The Tanunda Town Band was formed a year earlier than the *Liedertafel*, and it has functioned effectively ever since. Frequently father, son, and grandson served it in turn as sheet music and instruments were passed down from generation to generation.

The first Tanunda Band Competitions were held in October 1910, bands from near-by Nuriootpa, and from Freeling—just beyond the Valley to the north-west—taking part. The competitions lapsed during the first World War, but were resumed in 1920 and became famous throughout Australia. Every November large numbers of bands and spectators flocked to Tanunda, not only from the Valley (although Marananga, Nuriootpa, and Angaston gave stern competition) but from Adelaide and cities interstate.

A child's eye view of those days between the two World Wars was one of brass and glory: rows of marching legs seemingly glued together and moving with the unbelievable

Morning start at the
Band Competitions

precision of dozens of pairs of scissors, shattering tuckets of trumpets like triumphant onslaughts on the walls of Jericho, huge tubas grunting along with a kind of elephantine exuberance, the passionate involvement of the spectators, the spit and polish of boots and brass, the splendour of caps, braid, and epaulets, the excruciating erectness of the band masters shrilling piercingly on huge silver whistles inscribed "Acme Thunderer," and semaphoring with arms as rigid as railway signals, and the spectacular mass performances on the Tanunda oval where the bands marched and countermarched in tight squares as if Wellington and Blücher were deploying their forces for a new Waterloo.

But it was all superbly done—quality of music sought after no less than precision of movement. And today the tradition remains unbroken still.

But music went beyond *Liedertafel* and Town Band in community life. It was an integral part of worship, an expression of faith. From the pastor's liturgical chant to the congregation's lusty singing of the hymns, from the metallic accompaniment of brass instruments in church to the choral mellowness of pipe organ and choir, music and religion went hand in hand. It buttressed faith, provided defence in adversity, especially through the conviction of the old hymns —the solid assurance of *Ein feste Burg ist unser Gott*, the triumphant gratitude of *Nun danket alle Gott*.

Church services had their own ritual characteristics— some of them strange and contradictory to outside observers. Congregations sat for hymns, stood for prayers—the male and female components fiercely segregated on opposite sides of the aisle. And outside the church, before and after services, the men sat on their heels like elders of the tribe, in profound discussion of the vital issues confronting mankind: crops and weather, soil and stubble, yields and prices, tools and labour. Although the Barossa grew no boree logs, it certainly had its counterparts of the Hanrahans and Nelsons.

THE CHURCHES

Lutheran Pastor

The pastor was central to the community. He moved about actively among his parishioners, covering the most daunting distances on foot or by buggy in wind, rain, or summer dust, to serve distant congregations, to teach the catechism to confirmants, to officiate at baptisms, weddings, and funerals. He was a venerable figure at the Sunday services in sweeping black robes with wide sleeves and starched white *Bäffchen*. And he was usually a powerful and uncompromising preacher.

The early congregations had a liking for overhead pulpits built high against the front wall of the church and served by a private staircase and door. Here the pastor could materialize suddenly out of the wall like a cuckoo to admonish his people.

The pulpits were not always wise innovations structurally, especially with heavy or histrionic preachers, and one, at least, came close to precipitating its pastor down on the upturned faces of his flock.

The church history of the Barossa is highly involved, almost every congregation having undergone complex changes. But the thirty-six Lutheran church buildings they produced are distinctive, and most are as well-kept and vigorously used today as they ever were. Apart from Bethany and Langmeil, it is hard to say whether one church is historically more important than another. Any choice, therefore, must tend to be personal and arbitrary. Nevertheless it is interesting to visit perhaps a half dozen, if only to notice the minor differences in design—and the major similarities.

The beginnings of Bethany were complex. In 1839 Charles Flaxman, agent in South Australia for George Fife Angas, ignored his master's explicit instructions and bought 28,000 acres of land in the Gawler River area at one pound an acre. He then offered 2,080 acres of this to the incoming German settlers at ten pounds an acre. The proposal was accepted at the first Lutheran synod in Australia at Glen Osmond, and a formal contract was signed on 30 June 1839.

However, many of the families already living at Klemzig, Hahndorf, and Glen Osmond refused to act on the decision

Altar Vessels

of their delegates and the agreement lapsed. Subsequently Angas offered parcels of land for private purchase by individual German farmers; some accepted, and small groups began moving north to "Neu-Schlesien" soon afterwards. In this way Bethany (Bethanien) was founded in 1842, and Langmeil in 1843.

Bethany was the first Lutheran settlement in the Valley. Until recently its communal organization could still be traced in some of the fences that ran back in straight lines from the main road to the Tanunda Creek, and which originally divided the settlement into narrow field strips in the ancient European tradition. There was common pasture land too, on the eastern uplands near Mengler's Hill where the ranger or shepherd, having rounded up the cattle at night for milking, blew a blast on his horn that could be heard clearly in the village below. And true to the spirit of the commune the tolling of the church bell at sunset signalled the end of work for the day.

The Langmeil settlement was less compact, although corporate feeling was still strong and religious gatherings dominated community life. The early services were held "in private homes"—small, low-walled, thatched cottages of post and daub, stone and pug. Pastor Kavel had to travel the 40 miles each way from Klemzig on horseback or by cart to officiate. It wasn't until 1846, when a church incorporating living quarters for the pastor had been erected, that Kavel actually came to live at Langmeil. His name has been associated with it ever since.

The first church was a low stone rectangle with a straw roof and no ceiling. It was unsatisfactory, and constant improvements followed: by 1856 the pastor's rooms had become part of the church, porches had been added to the entrance, and a bell had been hung in a near-by gum tree. In the same year the brass instruments which had accompanied the hymn singing gave way to an organ. Three years later an iron roof replaced the straw, £100 being borrowed from Angas at 10% to pay for it.

Pastor Kavel died on 12 February 1860, and he was buried in the Langmeil cemetery adjacent to the church. About 1,500 people attended the funeral, and fine written tributes were paid to him by the Governor and prominent citizens. Immediately after his death Langmeil and most of the other churches in the Valley were wracked by intense doctrinal discord which led to widespread shifts of membership. Langmeil's numbers fell dramatically. Despite this, the congregation (numbering only seventy) decided to demolish the old church in 1888 and erect a new one "of such a size that the inhabitants of Tanunda were astounded." J. Basedow was the builder, using fine stone from a quarry to the east of Bethany; the foundations were laid on 25 July 1888, and the completed church was dedicated four months later, on 25 November. Apart from the addition of an apse and a new vestry in 1938, and minor subsequent alterations, this is substantially the church we see today. The long approach through cypress pines and cemetery headstones makes it one of the most striking in the Valley, just as its early association with Pastor Kavel makes it historically the most important.

Ebenezer Church door.

The establishment of Ebenezer was a good example of migrants settling *en masse*. On 24 November 1851, the 400 ton barque *Helene* arrived at Port Adelaide with about 150 emigrants on board. Of these, two thirds were Wends from Saxony, about seventy of whom moved north in a body into the Hundred of Belvidere and formed a compact settlement which they called Ebenezer.

Soon afterwards new waves of migrants pushed out towards the Moppa Hills and Koonunga, along the valley of the Greenock Creek, and north-easterly towards Truro and Dutton. The whole district became very closely settled—too much so for successful farming there—and a second congregation established itself. This was Neukirch (the "Dimchurch" of the surveyor's maps) so named after a hamlet near Goldberg in Silesia.

Both congregations dedicated churches almost simultaneously: Ebenezer on 13 February 1859, and Neukirch on 29 May of the same year. The latter still stands today (with a porch added and an iron roof replacing the thatch)—the third oldest Lutheran church building still in use in Australia.

Ebenezer Church.

Church Altar.

The Ebenezer building gave long service too, but by the end of the century the thatched roof was leaking so badly that the members decided to rebuild completely. This is the church of today, dedicated in April 1905. The bell, originally housed in a belfry in the yard, still tolls from its tower as resonantly as ever, its lip deeply indented by the clapper; and the unique little pipe organ, built in 1875, is still in use too in its gallery at the head of the near-vertical staircase.

Despite its unpretentiousness, this district at the northern end of the Valley has seen important events. Not least was the beginning of the Riverina Trek, when fifty-six people in fourteen covered waggons and two carts set out on an 800 mile migration along the Murray on 13 October 1868, to make new homes near Albury. The caravan left from the house of Johann Mickan, about three quarters of a mile east of Ebenezer church, and eventually established Walla Walla in New South Wales. It was at Ebenezer, too, that the historic Synod was held in 1921 which brought the United Lutheran Church of Australia into being—an event commemorated by a large memorial stone in the churchyard.

The exact origins of the Gnadenfrei church at Marananga were probably lost when Pastor Kavel's private records were destroyed. It is almost certain that at first it formed part of the Langmeil (Tanunda) group, but at some time between 1850 and 1853 its members hived off, though they were still served by Kavel. The name itself, spelled *Gnadenfrey* in the early references, was probably taken from the town of that name near Reichenbach in Upper Silesia.

Gnadenfrei was deeply affected by the great rifts that shook the Lutheran Church in the 1860s. (The basic issues

Gnadenfrei – Marananga.

were Kavel's chiliastic doctrines, his protestations against Lutheran Confessions, and his rigid insistence on the validity of his "apostolic constitution." Pastor G. W. Staudenmayer, who came to South Australia as Kavel's assistant in 1857, opposed most of these views, and the parishioners themselves were sharply divided.) At the Langmeil Synod of 1860, when a large part of the congregation withdrew to form St John's, Tanunda, Gnadenfrei also separated itself from Langmeil, although individual families remained loyal. This kind of split allegiance accounted for the remarkable geographical distribution of congregational loyalties in the Barossa Valley during the century that followed.

As usual, an early and more primitive building served Gnadenfrei in the early years, but in 1873 the present church was built. With lime costing seven pence a bushel, masons Hoffmann and Ullrich erected it "at the contract price of 3/6 a yard." Significant donations came from beyond its own membership, notably from G. F. Angas, H. J. Angas,

Hand embroidered Vestment in Bethingrove Chapel.

and B. Seppelt. Forty years later the building was extended and the tower added—a striking piece of Norman architecture with a crest and bellchamber like a crown held poised for coronation.

Tabor in Tanunda (on the opposite side of the main street from Langmeil) was another one of the Valley's early churches. It was rebuilt in 1871 and again in 1910 when the present tower was added. It is eighty-six feet high, houses three bells, and is surmounted by the symbolic orb and cross taken from the old 1871 church. Tabor is unique in that the early records of the congregation, instead of being placed under the foundation stone in the customary way, were sealed in the orb and mounted on top of the spire.

The early settlers in the eastern and south-eastern areas of the Valley, especially the Parrot Hill district near Moculta (1856-57), were almost all pioneers who had first settled at Bethany and felt a strong spiritual allegiance there. But the twelve-mile cross-country walk to church every Sunday was a little too far, they thought—especially for the younger children. And so, in 1858, they decided to build their own church, the site being selected by drawing lots to resolve local jealousies. This was Gnadenberg.

Because the farmers were very poor the building was erected communally—stones quarried, sand carted, beams and roofing timbers (as they remain today) sawn from local redgum. The roof was straw thatch, the floor tamped earth, the forms hard and backless (also made of local redgum). These backless benches and the communal snuff-box which was passed from neighbour to neighbour during the service were, according to a later preacher, "a real smack in the eye for Satan" in his efforts to lull members to sleep during the sermon. Indeed, the preacher's thunderous oratory, the

Kavels Memorial

Collingrove Chapel.

congregation's explosive sneezes, and the general mortification of the flesh in aching backs and buttocks made Sunday the most memorable day of the week.

But inevitably improvements followed. By 1880 a floor had been laid, the benches had become pews, and galvanized iron on the roof meant that the listeners could no longer admire the rays of sunlight streaming through the thatch—like balks and golden planks. In 1897 a stone stable and chaff shed were erected at the church for the pastor's horses, and in 1904 the tower was added. An appeal to the German Kaiser, Friedrich Wilhelm II, inviting him to donate the metal for the bell, having been declined, one of the parishioners offered to do it instead. The bell was cast at the famous Apolda foundry in Thueringen—its landed cost in South Australia: sixty pounds.

Although the headstones in the little cemetery near by are a tragic memorial to the shocking infant and child mortality rate of the early years, and though the congregation underwent many administrative and doctrinal vicissitudes, the church still stands firmly today on the uplands of its grace.

Collingrove Homestead
-Angaston

Not all the early places of worship were Lutheran. The beautiful little Collingrove chapel, for example, was originally Baptist. It was erected a few hundred yards east of Collingrove homestead in 1874 by John Howard Angas, the majority of the seventy members of the first congregation coming from Collingrove itself. The employees there probably had to "attend chapel" as a matter of course. In 1906 the building was rededicated as a Church of England, the memorial apse to John Howard Angas being added at the same time. It was John Howard, too, who had erected the large memorial with its historic inscriptions, at the Angas family vault a mile or two away.

The Collingrove Chapel has never been the property of the Church, but has always remained part of the Angas estate. Today it is used only for family occasions, the carefully preserved altar cloths and vessels being brought across from the Collingrove homestead for each ceremony.

Palms

THE WINEMAKERS

Although religion is at the heart of local life, and church spires prick the gentle air in all directions, they are not the most dominant outward aspect of the landscape. The real pattern of the Valley is the vineyard: an all-pervading impression of greenness in summer and symmetry in winter. The superb precision of the vineyard rows is something that moves even the most unmathematical of visitors. The folding slopes are given an orderliness, a geometrical fitness, that seems to accord with the character and background of the people; marching vineyards and marching bandsmen — the discipline of order imposed on man and nature for the good government of both.

The roots of the wine industry go deep. "I am satisfied that New Silesia will furnish the province with such a

Old Press

quantity of wine that we shall drink it as cheap as in Cape Town," wrote Johann Menge to George Fife Angas in 1840. Menge, a German geologist, was camped in a cave near Jacob's Creek when he made his prediction. And he was right. The Barossa has come to be synonymous with wine—in imagination and in fact. Nearly 20,000 acres of vines and twenty-three wineries are there now, the core of the industry in a State that produces over two thirds of Australia's wine.

Most of the first beginnings date from 1847. In that year Johann Gramp, a German migrant who had already been in the colony for ten years, planted vines near Jacob's Creek. He produced his first wine in 1850. It was in 1847, too, that Joseph Gilbert, who had taken out a special survey at Pewsey Vale, put in his acre of vineyard; and in the same year Samuel Hoffmann, another German, settled near Tanunda with his eight sons and gradually switched from farming to grape-growing. In 1847, yet again, Samuel Smith arrived in South Australia from Dorsetshire, and two years later planted his first vineyard near Angaston. And in 1850 Joseph Seppelt migrated out of Germany and soon afterwards began his plantings at Seppeltsfield. They were all tenuous beginnings but like the vine itself, the idea took root and spread. The Barossa wine industry with its tradition of family enterprise was under way.

Inevitably it developed its own individuality—the pickers in the vineyards, the high-sided German waggons, the presses, vats, and stills, the autumn odour when the whole Valley seemed to have fermentation on its breath, and the specialized skills of a highly specialized product, from pruner to taster, cooper to chemist.

Nothing is more romantically linked with wine than the cooperage: puncheons, pipes, casks, and hogsheads; staves, hoops, bungs, and taps. It's all a miracle of skill, a product of pandemonium. No wonder the coopers wear earplugs or risk deafness. But despite the constant crash of mallet and hammer, there is something superb about the way the curved staves move into place and lock together so perfectly in the finished cask, that its precious contents can breathe yet never ooze to waste. And all the hand tools still hold their place in such craftsmanship, no less than the men who wield them. There was a time recently when some people predicted that stainless steel, plastic, and mechanization were ready to make an end of the cooper, but the virtues of wood and human skill remain: "faithfully aged in oak" is a slogan that lives.

This is not to say that changes in the industry have not been immense. It is a far cry from the hand-press and the backyard cellar of a century ago, to the sophisticated wine-maker of today. The oenologist, the chemist, the laboratory research worker have moved in, and all stages of wine-making are under closer scrutiny and control than ever before. For all that, there is still something deliberate about winemaking at its best. "Patience is the indispensable thing," says Wyndham Hill Smith of Yalumba, and most men in the Valley agree that it is a good creed for wine-makers to live by. There is much about the industry too that is unshakably traditional; although the German waggons have gone from the vineyards, grape-picking will always need deft hands and strong backs. The German women of the Valley—bonneted and scarved, ham-fisted and piston-armed—may no longer dominate the scene as they did in Max Harris's "Wordsworth in Barossa":

> *Behold yon social Silesian lass,*
> *With her plaits and apron, dirndl, draught-horse*
>   *thighs,*
> *Sitting on top of the sloping German waggon,*
> *Sighing and creaking and rolling her eyes . . .*

But there are still plenty of women pickers strung out along the rows in March and April, especially on the holdings of the small private growers. And there are 450 of those.

German Waggon.

Cooperage - Tanunda

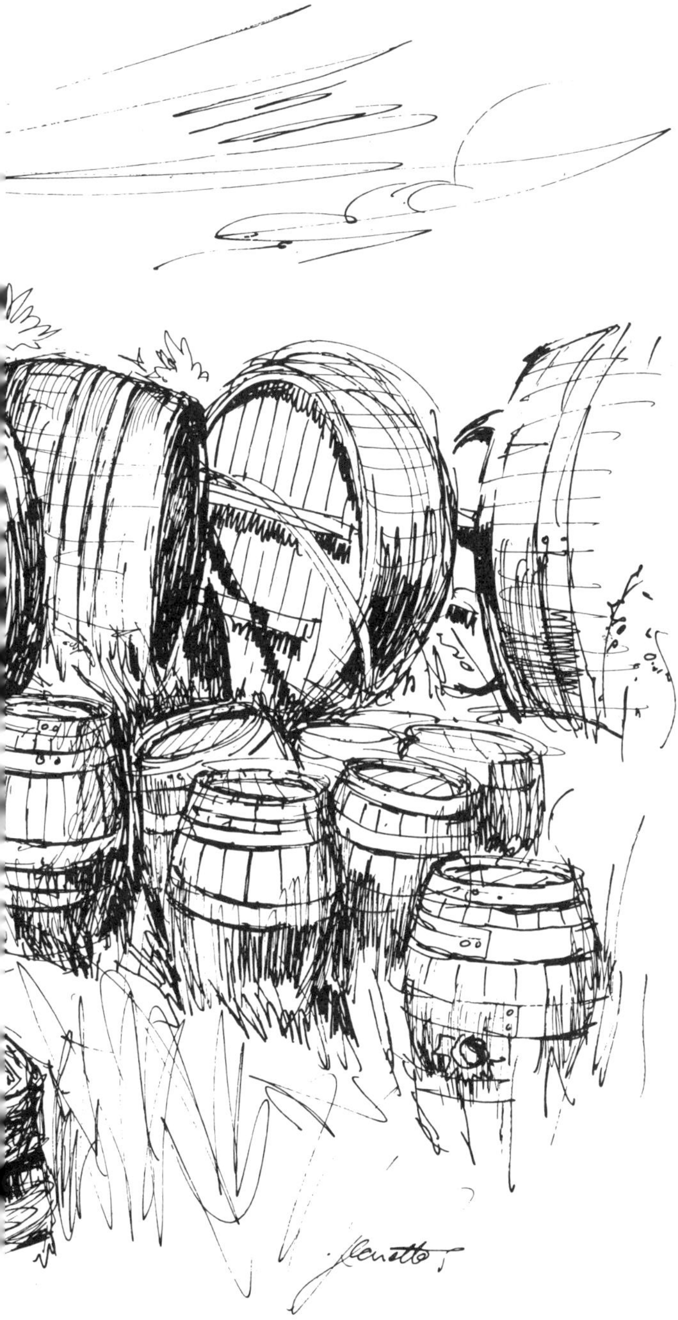

The strong predilection for family enterprise in the industry is borne out most clearly in the great wineries. Gramp, Smith, Seppelt, Hoffmann, Henschke, Basedow . . . the names read like a Who's Who of Australian wine. Most of them can trace direct links through four or five generations. Old Johann Gramp, for example, who planted his first vines at Jacob's Creek in 1847 and laboriously pressed out one octave of hock-type wine by hand in 1850, was laying the foundations of Orlando. In 1877 his eldest son, Gustav, took over and moved to the present site at Rowland Flat. And so the line went on. The tragic death of Hugo Gramp (managing director of the limited company that had been formed in 1912) in the Kyeema air crash in 1938, did not break it; today Fred Gramp presides over an organization that has a storage capacity of four million gallons.

It was likewise with Samuel Smith who fathered Yalumba. A dour Dorset brewer whose only apparent recreation was churchgoing, he planted his first tiny vineyard near Angaston, by moonlight, because during the day he was busy working as a gardener at Lindsay Park—Angas's colonial mansion—near by. Samuel went off to the Bendigo goldfields in 1852 with the express purpose of making enough money to buy more land for vines. He was back a few months later and added eighty acres to the thirty he had already. By the time he died in 1888, aged seventy-six, he had established the basis of Yalumba. His son, Sidney, developed it further. It was he who put up the two-storey building we know today, with its blue marble walls and its square towers, as solid in character as old Samuel himself.

Sidney's sons, Percival and Walter, carried on the tradition, Walter becoming the first managing director when the business was formed into a limited private company in 1923. He travelled prodigiously, and was such a relentless big game hunter that his trophies still decorate the homes of his descendants. When he died in 1938 his son Sid Hill Smith took over, but a few months later he was killed in the same Kyeema air disaster that took the lives of Hugo Gramp and Tom Hardy. Wyndham Hill Smith, the

present managing director, then took over, and he has
carried out the big expansion programme that has marked
Yalumba since the 1950s. An extraordinarily versatile man—
artist, first-class cricketer, race-horse owner, general sports-
man, and volatile conversationalist—he was a member of
the syndicate which bought Lindsay Park in 1965, for the
purpose of creating one of Australia's greatest racing studs.
The beautiful 800 acre property with its tree-studded
paddocks and its magnificent old mansion, which was for
years one of the show places of the State, has now become a
place of white fences, stables, training track, and home of
magnificently bred stallions. The wheel seems to have
turned full circle since old Samuel tended the gardens there
in 1847.

Each winery has its own story. The five generations of Hoffmanns begin with Samuel, a veteran of Waterloo who migrated to South Australia in 1847. A century of Henschke family life has gone into the Keyneton vineyards on the eastern uplands beyond the Valley; four generations of Basedows have trodden the rows of the Illapara vineyards at Tanunda; and Ernest Tolley founded the organization that runs three big brandy and wine establishments today. Penfold's first association with the Valley was less direct, the company buying grapes there and railing them to Magill for processing. But in 1913 it began to set up its own plant in Nuriootpa, culminating in a 5,000 gallon still, the biggest pot still operating in Australia at that time, for producing rectified spirit and brandy. After the first World War the Penfold organization also built a distillery at Eden Valley, 16 miles east of Nuriootpa, to take in local grapes from the Springton area; and after the second World War expansion and modernization led to enormously increased production, and to scientific research in well-equipped laboratories. Buring, too, was another great name that came to the Valley later.

Burings

Yalumba

One of the best known of all the family names is the house of Seppelt, begun by Joseph Seppelt when, having planted vines and tobacco plants simultaneously, he took up the success of the one as shrewdly as he wrote off the failure of the other. By the time of his death in 1868, Seppeltsfield was becoming something of a show place.

But it was Joseph's son, Benno, a young man of twenty-one when his father died, who really built the Seppelt empire. Hard-working and abstemious, thoughtful, inventive, and extraordinarily thorough, Benno Seppelt developed the family enterprise to a point that even his father would not have dreamt of. Constant improvement and expansion at Seppeltsfield itself, and widespread interest in new developments elsewhere, marked his era. And with thirteen children —nine boys and four girls—there was little danger of the organization ever lacking family representation. When vineyards in the eastern states were ravaged by phylloxera late in the century, South Australia was miraculously kept free of the disease, and the Barossa boomed. Early in the twentieth century, the family began developing new outlets and set up branches in most of the major cities of Australia. It also expanded production at home and interstate, by taking over the Clydeside vineyard and Rutherglen cellars in Victoria in 1914, by acquiring the famous Chateau Tanunda in 1916—an imposing building with a 240 foot bluestone façade and a sixty-four foot tower, built as one of the outstanding chateaux of the Valley in 1889; and finally by acquiring the Great Western champagne cellars near Ararat in 1918. By the time of Benno's death in 1930, at the age of eighty-five, the name of Seppelt was synonymous with wines, brandy, and champagne all over the nation.

The palm trees which are a characteristic landmark of all Seppelt wineries, and particularly of Seppeltsfield itself where they form an impressive avenue of approach, were planted at the instigation of Oscar Seppelt, one of Benno's sons, during the years of the great Depression. Apart from beautifying the area, the palm-planting programme provided

BRANDY STILL IN PENFOLDS WINERY

employment for staff who would otherwise have had to be retrenched.

There are also palms leading to the front of the Seppelt family mausoleum—a piece of pure Ionic Greek architecture, designed by J. G. Seppelt and built on a commanding hill site overlooking Seppeltsfield and the whole of the Barossa Valley.

Air, earth, and water; light and skyline, grass and furrow, orchard and vineyard; the straw-gold slopes of wheat and the silken green of the grapevine, the dip and swing of the hills, and the mauve-blue haze of distance . . . It is all there at one's feet, half Streeton, half Grüner. The forefathers of the Seppelts must sleep well in such a spot.

Storage Tanks at Seppeltsfield.

Seppelt's Mausoleum

Not all the wine-producing houses are old and long-established. Some, such as Chateau Yaldara, are excitingly recent. There, the master spirit—in the human sense—is H. Thumm, a German migrant who arrived in South Australia in 1947, exactly a hundred years after his great predecessors. He worked in a Valley winery for a year and then struck out on his own by taking over the shell of an old building near Lyndoch. In less than twenty years he made Chateau Yaldara one of the famous names of the Valley. Of course, as he himself admits, he sprang from many generations of wine-makers. "Wine is in our blood," he says with a smile; and then he tries to ensure, by hospitality

Seppelts

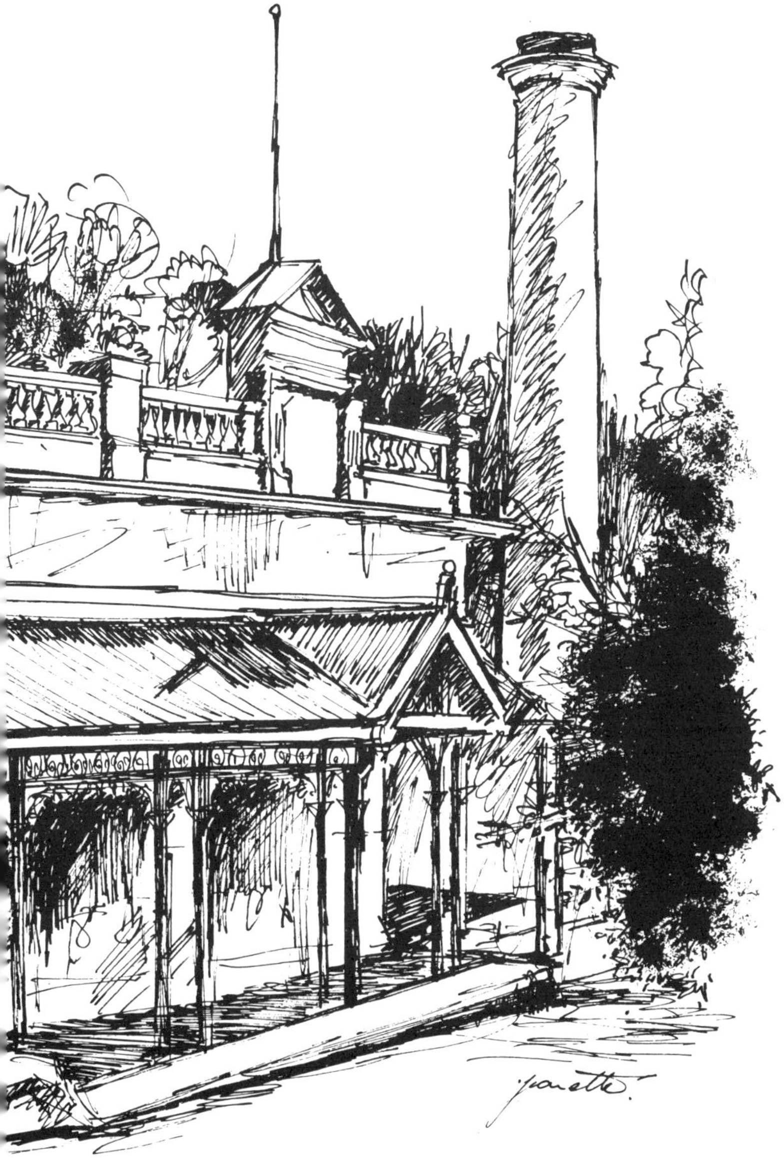

that has become legendary, that those who call on his chateau take away at least a little in theirs too. As his two sons begin to take over the responsibility for Yaldara, we see a new family line being established in the true tradition of the Barossa.

From early times the end of the vintage was marked by celebration—the secular counterpart of the religious festival of *Erntedankfest* (Harvest Thanksgiving). Most wineries, and even individual growers, organized functions of one kind or another as soon as the last bucket of grapes came in from the pickers or the last drop of juice was squeezed from the crushers. Seppeltsfield was renowned for it. On the night when the last waggon load came in, the acetylene lights were turned on everywhere and pickers, growers, and work-hands gathered from the surrounding district for the Seppelt celebrations. According to the centenary history of the family, published in 1951, "the big dining-hall was cleared, the fiddlers scraped until their arms were ready to drop off, the accordion players stretched their bellows and tapped time with their feet, and there was music, merriment and song far into the night."

Yaldara

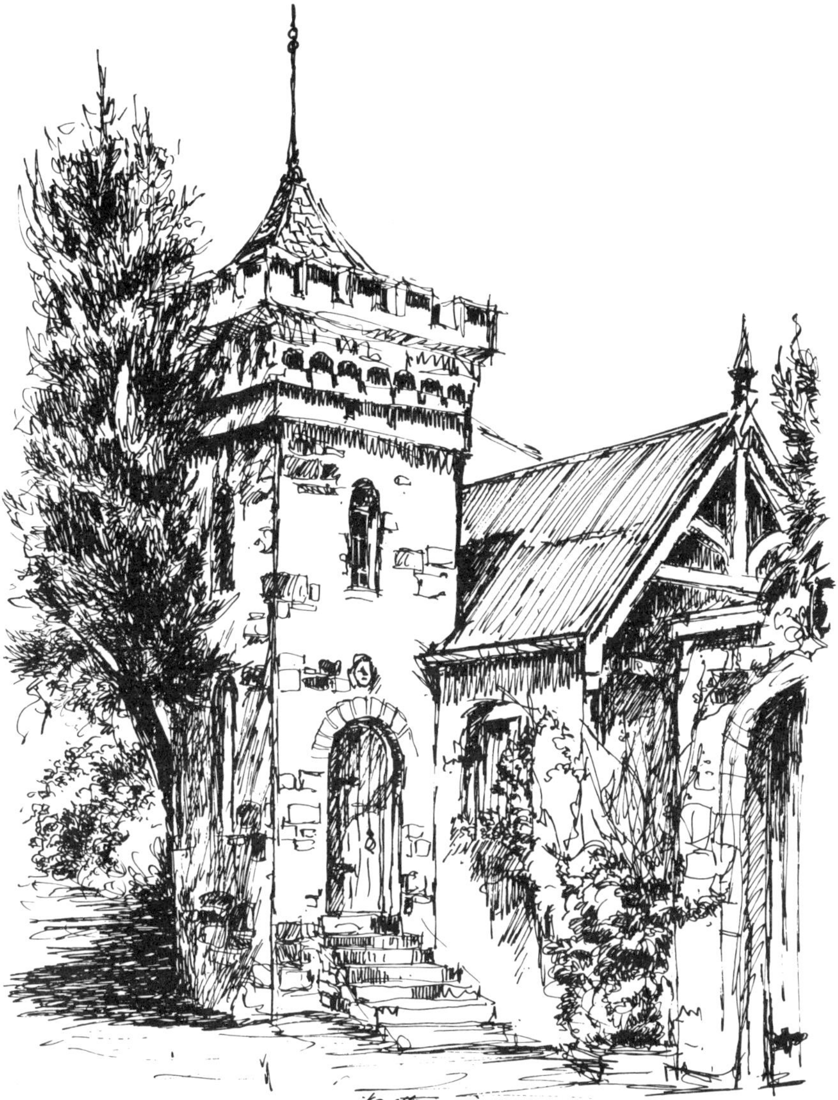

Maldara

It was a spirit for which the whole Valley soon became well known. Local rivalries between family and family, town and town tended to be forgotten in genuine gratitude for the natural largesse of the land—especially if the last days of the vintage had been a race against time and weather. Hail and tempest, high humidity, and summer rain were real threats that split open the berries and sent mildew and fungus racing through the syrupy bunches. Often the picking was finished against a deadline that posed such loss and ruin that young children were kept home from school and old grandmothers were pressed into service as pickers, to gather the grape in time. And so there was as much *Dank* as there was *Tanz* in the festivities that followed.

In later years the celebrations took on a broader tone which has culminated in the combined Vintage Festival of today. Flooded with visitors and tourists, the Valley promotes its reputation with much more than fiddles and song. The programme is likely to include everything from the crowning of a vintage queen to barrel-trundling competitions, to provide spectacle for the onlookers. And there are processions, grape-picking contests, marching bands, dancing in the streets, and a general yeasty spirit of merry-making in which wine-tasting is recognized as an art no less delicate than wine-making itself.

National Dance at Vintage Festival.

Yet in the midst of burgundy and beaune one must remember that the Valley has never been exclusively a vineyard. From the first, wheat was a major product; and fruit, vegetables, dairy cattle, and poultry have always flourished. Flour milling was an ancient art, the name of Laucke being deeply associated with it for generations. Laucke mills still grind away steadily at Greenock and Stockwell, the floors and ceilings seemingly thick with used-up years and the powder of sifted flour-dust. Krieg's brickyard was an early comer too. Appropriately it was a

Coulthard House
Nuriootpa.

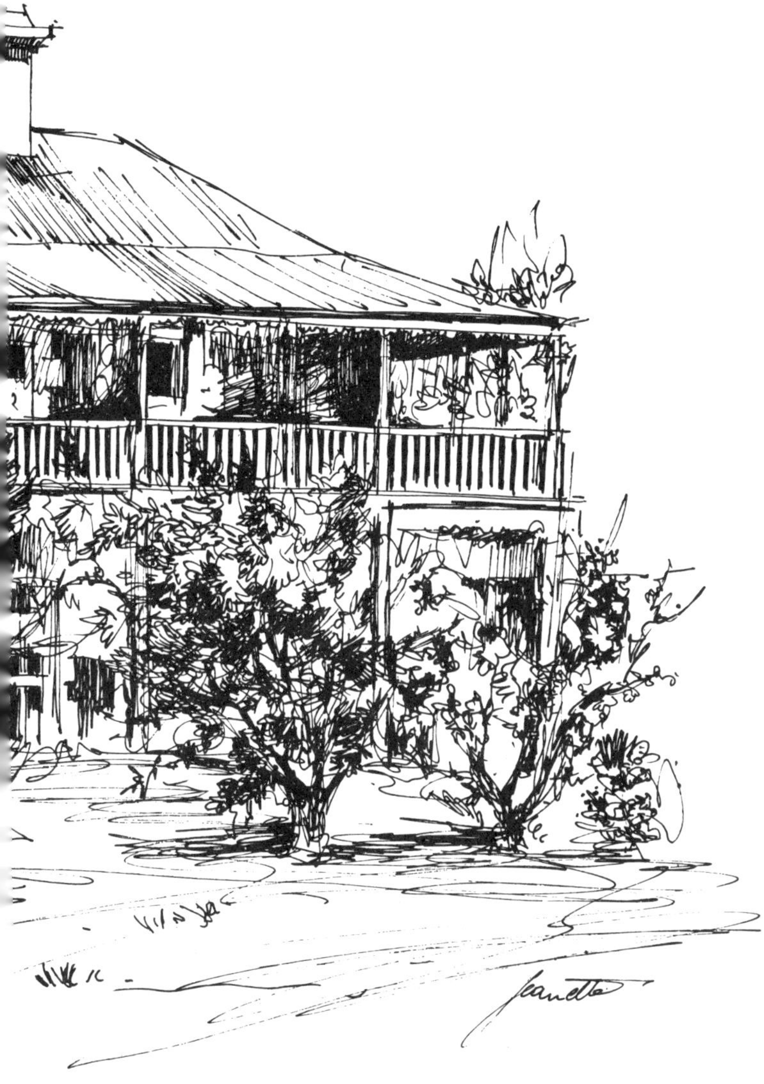

brickworks that also produced wine—one of the rarest combinations ever likely to be encountered in Australian industry. When Hermann Krieg began making bricks on his forty acre property at Nuriootpa in 1882, he found that the clay was only about a foot thick. He therefore pushed aside the top-soil carefully, carted the clay to his brickyard in the dray, and then replaced the soil and planted vines. Long before his supply of clay ran out he had a fine vineyard—and was making a superb dry sherry. Even today, one precious keg remains, a rare wine nurtured and tended by the third generation of brick-makers, periodically blended, heavy and mature, which only the most privileged brick-buyer may be allowed to sample.

The most famous of the celebrated homes of the Valley is Lindsay Park. But there are others. Coulthard House, now used as a hostel in the centre of Nuriootpa, commemorates William Coulthard, who moved into the area, then known as Angas Park, early in the 1840s. The discovery of copper at Kapunda in 1843, and the consequent traffic northwards

Inside Krieg's Brickyard.

Krieg's Brickyards – Nuriootpa.

from Adelaide, led him to build a hotel in what is now Nuriootpa, to catch the transit trade. Several Coulthard residences followed. House No. 1 and House No. 2 have disappeared, but House No. 3, probably built in 1906, still remains.

There are other old landmarks throughout the Valley: the original Tanunda Police Station and its outbuildings, the remnants of the old mileposts, bluestone houses, barns of a century ago, and the remains of the Tanunda tea-gardens. The Angaston Hotel, too, is a venerable hostelry—the first licence having been taken out by George Simpson on 24 December 1846; one can only presume that Christmas Eve was an appropriate and urgent time for such an application. The hotel underwent five stages of construction or reconstruction during the century that followed, although the basic present appearance of the building, particularly the

Angaston Hotel

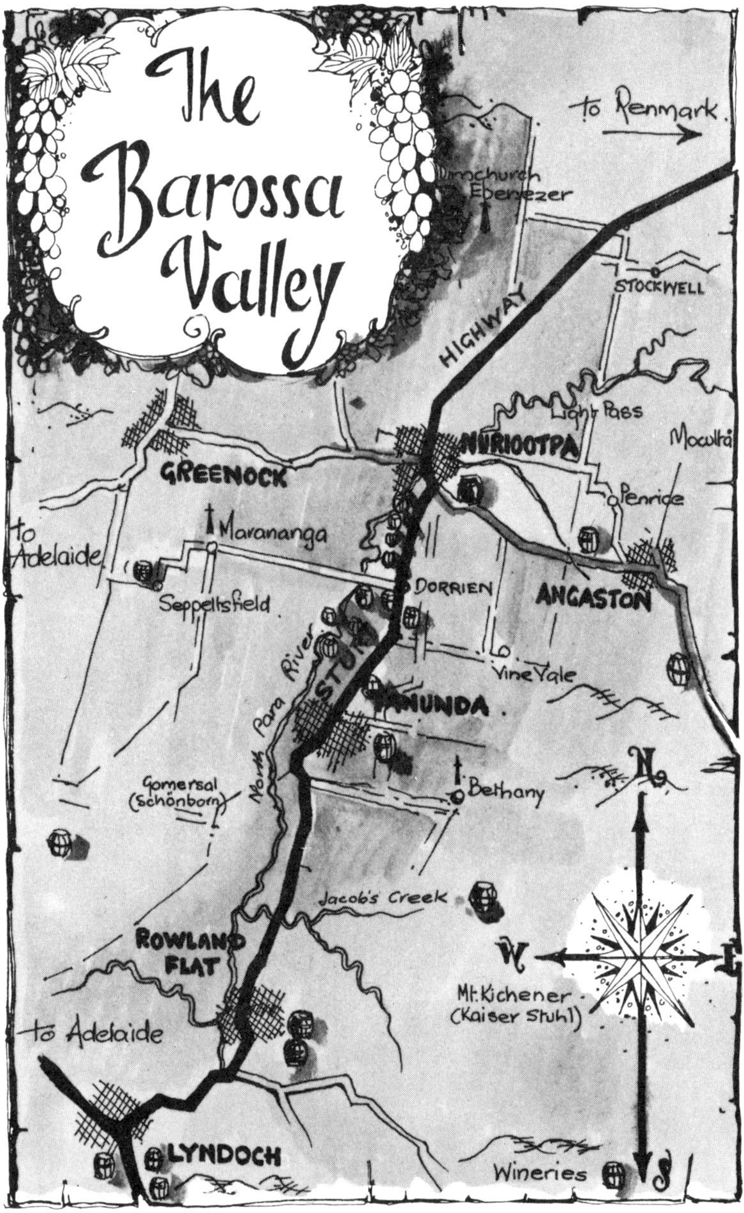
The Barossa Valley
to Renmark
Ebenezer
STOCKWELL
HIGHWAY
Light Pass
NURIOOTPA
Moculta
GREENOCK
Penrice
to Adelaide
Marananga
Seppeltsfield
DORRIEN
ANGASTON
North Para River
Vine Vale
Bethany
Gomersal (Schönborn)
N
W
E
S
Jacob's Creek
ROWLAND FLAT
Mt. Kichener (Kaiser Stuhl)
to Adelaide
LYNDOCH
Wineries

TANUNDA
Old Police Station

two-storey section, dates from 1914. The hotel proprietor, Frank Nicholls, has one of the finest collections of old drinking steins in the State, some of them over two hundred years old.

And so today, though change and convulsion wrack the world, the Barossa miraculously retains something of its old spirit. The scene remains rural. Man is at one with the earth, and the earth is good. Patience even yet is the indispensable thing. The cycle of the seasons, ploughing and vintage, worship and thanksgiving, birth and marriage, and birth again; the march of the vineyards and the march of the generations . . . It is all part of the Barossa even now.

"I am certain," Menge wrote to Angas in 1840, "that we shall see . . . vineyards and orchards and immense fields of corn throughout New Silesia, which is matchless in this colony." The prophecy was well justified, and has continued to be so ever since. If the old Lutheran migrants who fled Germany did not exactly find milk and honey, they and their descendants certainly found bread and wine.

It is no easy thing, nor ever was,
To set one's face for ever from the door,
Turn utterly away from a home's warmth
And walk the far strangeness of another shore.

Yet this they did, and bore that hard migration,
The rigour of a stern and stubborn goal,
That each might walk the way of his own choosing
And call himself to answer for his soul.

And, ageless as the alchemy of faith,
The granite-firm conviction of their wills,
Their ancient heritage sprang up anew
In the *dorfs* and *thals* enfolded in these hills.

Their mellow church-bells came to wring the air,
Their vines and pastures greened the earth they trod,
And in their daily labour and their love
They found their freedom here to find their God.

Colin Thiele
On the first Lutheran migrants to South Australia